the
dirty girl's
joke book

THIS IS A CARLTON BOOK

Text, illustrations, design copyright © 2003
Carlton Books Limited

This edition published by
Carlton Books Limited 2003
20 Mortimer Street
London W1T 3JW

A CIP catalogue record for this book is
available from the British Library
ISBN 1 84442 980 6

editorial manager: **Judith More**
art director: **Penny Stock**
executive editor: **Lisa Dyer**
editor: **Lara Maiklem**
design: **DW Design**
production controller: **Lucy Woodhead**
illustrator: **Anna Hymas**

Printed and bound in England

the
dirty girl's
joke book

CARLTON
BOOKS

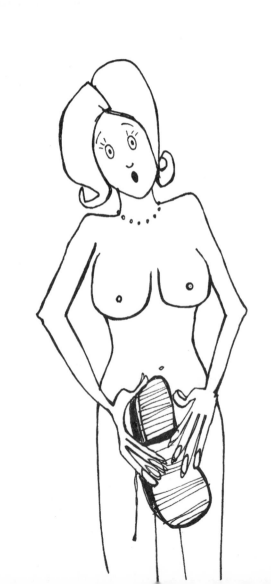

CONTENTS

Why do women fake orgasm?
Because men fake foreplay.

What does an **atheist** miss during orgasm?

Somebody to shout at.

How does a man make a woman scream in bed?
By wiping his dick on the curtains.

A little girl goes into **Santa's grotto** and he asks her what she wants for Christmas. 'I want **Barbie** and Action Man' she says. 'Oh,' says Santa, 'I thought Barbie came with Ken.' 'No,' says the little girl, 'Barbie **comes** with Action Man – she just **fakes it** with Ken.'

Do you know what your arsehole does when you have an orgasm?

He shouts, 'Hey, what's that buzzing noise coming from the bathroom?'

John says to his girlfriend, 'Why don't you shout my name out when you come?' **she answers, 'Yeah – like you're ever there when I come!'**

How do you know when you've given a **good** blow job?

He has to pull the bed sheets out of his arse.

A man walks into the bar and sees a sign – **'Win Free Drinks for Life'** – so he asks the barman how. 'Well,' says the barman, 'You have to pass three challenges. First, you have to drink a bottle of tequila. Next, the landlord's pit bull terrier out in the back yard has toothache – you have to go out and pull that tooth. Finally, the landlord's wife is upstairs and she's never had an orgasm – if you can do the business for her, you get free drinks for life.' So, the guy thinks he'll give it a try. He takes the bottle of tequila and downs it in one go. Then he staggers out into the back yard. There's terrible growling and snarling, and eventually the guy staggers back in, clawed and scratched all over but grinning from ear to ear. 'Right,' he says, 'that's the first two, now where's that lady with the toothache?'

Awoman and a man are riding together in a train. Suddenly, the woman sneezes, starts to writhe around and moan, quivers all over and then goes back to her book. After a few minutes the same thing happens, the sneeze, then the writhing, then the quivering. 'Are you all right?' asks the man. 'Yes,' says the woman, 'but I do have an unusual medical condition. Every time I sneeze, I have an automatic orgasm.' 'Are you taking anything for it?'asks the man. 'Yes, pepper,' she replies.

Woman goes into a shop and asks if they sell batteries. 'Yes, we have some in the back room' says the assistant, 'Come this way.' 'If I could come this way,' says the woman, 'I wouldn't need the batteries.'

How do you get a man in your bed, shouting your name and gasping for breath? **Hold a pillow over his face.**

Why is a woman like a police car?
They both make a lot of noise to let you know
they're coming.

Why is
sex
like
Eastenders?

**Just when it starts getting
interesting, it's all over for
another night.**

Why don't they let male porn stars work at petrol stations?

Because they always pull out the nozzle at the last minute and spray petrol all over your windscreen.

A woman meets a German in a bar and goes back to his hotel room. He confides that he's a bit kinky, and would she mind dressing up? She says no, so he gets out a big costume, covered in feathers, with a duck's bill and big webbed feet. She thinks this is ok, so she puts it on and they start shagging. Then he then asks if she would mind putting something else on, and gets out four huge bedsprings. She says ok, so he straps them on her knees and elbows, she gets on all fours and soon they're at it, bouncing away, getting more and more excited.

Finally, he asks her if she'll shout 'Quack! Quack!' As soon as she does this, they both have the most amazing orgasm. 'How did you do that?' she asks, as soon as she can speak. **'Four-sprung duck technique'** he replies.

BOY'S
BITS

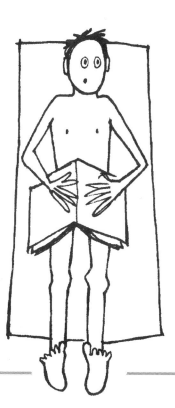

A man goes into a party shop

and says, 'I'd like to hire a costume, I'm going to a fancy dress party as Adam.' So the assistant gets out a fig leaf, 'There you are sir, that's £5.' 'No, that's not big enough,' he says, so she gets out a bigger one. 'That one's £10.' 'Still not big enough,' he says, so she gets out an even bigger one. 'This one's £15,' she says. 'No, I won't fit into that,' he says, so she gets out a hat that says Esso. 'There,' she says, 'wear this, sling it over your shoulder and go as a petrol pump.'

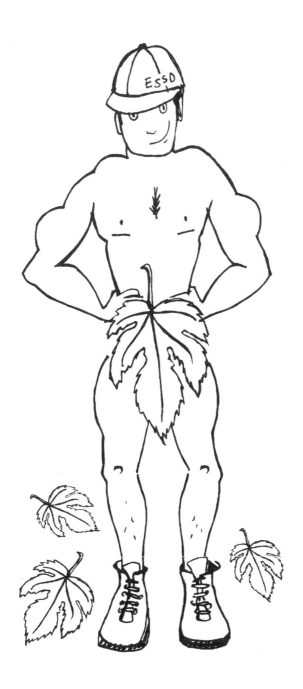

What's the definition of a man with a small penis?

If he walks into a door with an erection he bangs his nose.

Man goes into a chemist and asks **'Do you sell Viagra?'**
'Yes,' says the chemist.
'And does it work?'
'Yes,' says the chemist.
'And can you get it over the counter?'
'Yes, if I take two.'

Heard about the new Viagra eye drops?
They make him look really hard.

Who's the most popular man on the nudist beach?

The one who can carry **two** cups of coffee and **six** doughnuts.

Who's the most popular girl on the nudist beach?

The one who can eat the sixth doughnut.

How do you get some groovy lovin'?

Use a corduroy condom.

Why did God give men pricks? So women would have a reason to talk to them.

What's the difference between anal sex and a microwave?

A microwave can't turn your meat brown.

A man goes into a chemist and asks for something that will keep him **hard all night**, as he has a hot date with twin sisters, so the chemist gives him a tube of stay-hard cream. Next day, he's back in the chemist, walking a bit strangely, and asking for a tube of **muscle rub**. 'You don't want to put muscle rub on your penis,' says the chemist. 'It's not for my penis,' says the man. 'The twin sisters never showed up so this is for my wrist.'

One day Bill noticed that his penis had started growing.

He was delighted as it rapidly reached six inches, eight inches, then ten inches – and so was his wife. By the time it reached twenty inches, however, Bill was finding it difficult to walk, so they went to see a doctor.

The doctor examined Bill and said that he could carry out corrective surgery. Bill's wife looked worried at this. 'But Doctor,' she says, 'How long will Bill be in a wheelchair?'

'Dear lady,' says the doctor, 'Why should he be in a wheelchair?' 'Well, Doctor,' she replies, 'You are going to lengthen his legs, aren't you?'

Hear about the man with five pricks?
His underpants fit like a glove.

A penis has a sensitive part at one end – called the glans – and an insensitive part at the other – called a man.

A woman calls a male escort agency and asks for the most mind-blowing sex she's ever had. They say they'll send over their best stud, Ramon. A while later, the doorbell rings but when she answers the door, she sees a man with no arms and no legs down on the floor. 'I am Ramon,' says the man. 'You?' says the woman, 'How can you give me the most mind-blowing sex I've ever had? You've got no arms and no legs.' 'Listen, lady,' says Ramon, 'I rang the doorbell, didn't I?'

A man finds a genie in a bottle, and is offered three wishes. First he asks for a sports car and bouf! There's a shiny red car. Then he asks for a big luxurious house and bouf! There's a huge mansion. Finally he asks to be made irresistible to women. Bouf! He turns into a box of chocolates.

Two nuns are sitting on a bench when a streaker **runs past. One has a stroke, but the other one can't reach.**

How does a bloke make up his mind?

He puts mascara on his bollocks.

How can you spot a blind man on a nudist beach?

It's not hard.

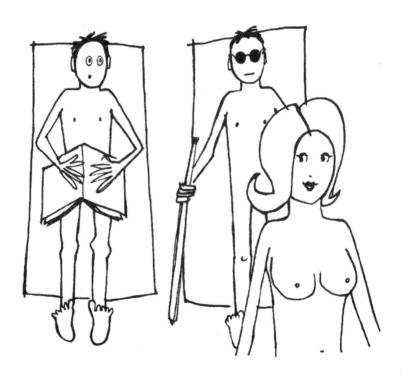

According to women, pricks come in three sizes: Small, medium and ohmigod.

According to men, there are still three sizes: large, average and size-doesn't-matter.

Why is a man like a Swiss Army Knife?
He's meant to have a useful and versatile tool, but he spends most of his time just opening beer.

A girl takes a guy home. When he takes his pants off, he's got the biggest cock she's ever seen – it reaches down past his knees. 'You want a blow job?' she says, but he replies, 'I'd rather fuck, I can do blow jobs myself.'

Why is it dangerous to take Viagra and iron tablets?

Every time he gest an erection he ends up pointing North.

Why does an elephant have four feet?

Six inches would look silly on an elephant.

What's the difference between Niagara and Viagra?

Niagara Falls.

What's the definition of stealing Viagra?

A hold-up by hardened criminals.

What do you get if you cross a penis and a potato?

A dictator.

A couple meet in a bar and end up back at his place. 'You don't talk much,' she says as he's undressing. 'No,' he says, 'I do my talking with this.' 'Sorry,' she says, 'I don't do small talk.'

Want to come back to my place?
Will both of us fit under the one rock?

Your place or mine?
Both, you go to yours and I'll
go to mine.

What's your sign?
No Entry.

If I could see you naked,
I could die happy.
**Yeah? If I saw you
naked, I'd die laughing.**

Word of the day is **'legs'** – come back to my place and let's spread the word.

Come back when you have enough words for a whole sentence.

I seem to have lost my phone number, can I have yours?

It's okay, I've already got your number.

You know, I like an intelligent woman.

Yeah, I heard opposites attract.

Women can't read maps.

Well only a man would think an inch equals a mile.

If your tits were a bit firmer, you wouldn't need that bra.
If your cock was a bit firmer, I wouldn't need your brother.

Am I the first man you ever made love to?
You might be – your face looks familiar.

Want to suck it?

Sorry, I **choke** on small bones.

Haven't I seen you before?
**Yes, I'm the receptionist
from the VD clinic.**

When men say,
'Do you have any fantasies?'
they mean, 'Can we try anal sex/you dressing up as Batgirl/a threesome with your sister?'
When women say,
'Do you have any fantasies?'
they mean, 'I'm so bored that, frankly, I'll try anything.'

When men say,
'Who else do you fancy?'
they mean, 'I fancy your sister.'
When women say,
'Who else do you fancy?'
they mean, 'you fancy my sister, don't you?'

4

POINTS
TO
REMEMBER

Why is a bicycle better than a man?

1. You can ride your bicycle for as long as you like, and it won't get there before you do.

2. A bicycle never complains at having to wear rubber tyres.

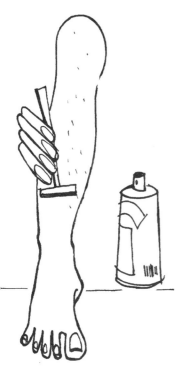

3. You don't have to shave your legs before you go out on your bicycle.

4. Your parents won't go on about how much they liked your old bicycle.

5. Nothing goes soft on a bicycle that a bicycle pump won't fix.

What are the **ten** worst things about being a **penis**?

1. Your next door neighbour is an arsehole.

2. You can't get excited without wanting to throw up.

3. Every time you get all relaxed, someone

takes your sleeping bag away.

4. You're bald all your life but with really hairy feet.

5. You've always got two nuts hanging around you.

6. Your home is pants.

7. In cold weather you shrink.

8. You've only got one eye.

9. Every time your owner remembers you're there, he tries to strangle you.

10. Women would rather see you stiff.

Ten things not to say **to a naked man:**

1. Is it really that size, or are you standing a long way away?

2. Oh, are we skipping straight to the cigarette?

3. Very funny, now put the real one back on.

4. I hope your tongue is bigger than that.

5. Oh well, no hard feelings.

6. And what does it want to be when it grows up?

7. You know, maybe we should go fishing instead?

8. And your shoes were so huge.

9. Still, no danger of a gag reflex tonight.

10. Never mind, if we plant it maybe a great oak will grow.

If men had a **vagina** for a **day** they would:

1. Wonder what the little pink button next to it does.
2. Lie in bed all morning with a hand mirror.
3. Get up and go shopping for cucumbers.

4. Go to church and pray for breasts as well.

5. Secretly worry about whether it was bigger than everybody else's.

6. Lie in bed all afternoon with a home video camera.

7. Finally find that damn g-spot the all the fuss is about.

8. Get picked up in a bar without even trying.

9. Have an orgasm – then have another one without needing a nap first.

10. Repeat number 9.

If women **had a** penis **for a** day they **would:**

1. Measure it to see whether that really is six inches.

2. Pee standing up, without even trying to hit the toilet.

3. Get a blow job.

4. Fall asleep without saying thanks.

5. Wake up.

6. Repeat number 3.

7. Repeat number 3.

8. Repeat number 3.

9. Repeat number 3.

10. Repeat number 3.

Why are **dogs** better than men?

1. If a dog wants to go out, it will let you know.

2. A dog will express affection in public.

3. A dog will play ball without telling you how to throw overarm.

4. You can train a dog to understand what 'no' means.

5. If a dog wants its balls licked, it will do it for itself.

6. After six months, a dog will still look excited to see you.

7. Just because you've had some fun with a dog, it doesn't think it can sleep on your bed.

8. Dogs feel guilt.

9. Dogs are grateful when you stroke them.

10. When your dog gets old, you can just get a younger dog.

Cars are better than **sex** because:

1. You get a manual with your car – 'Sudden failure of big end? Wait for excess alcohol to drain out of system. Turnover rate too rapid? Clean all points of contact with a wire brush.'

2. Your car is insured against accidental injury to a third party – 'Dear Madam, with

regards to your claim, our client says that your husband went straight into her rear while she was stationary and waiting to enter a box junction – therefore she cannot accept any responsibility.'

3. If your Escort has an accident, they will lend you a replacement while they fix it – the replacement is usually faster, younger and shinier.

4. A car doesn't need emotional maintenance, just a drop of oil every month or so.

STAYING
TOGETHER

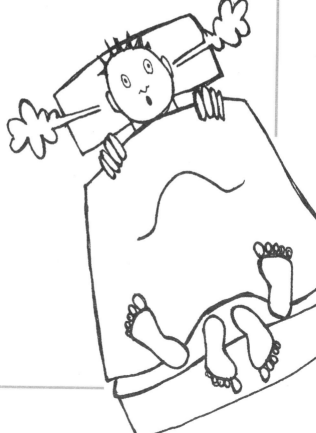

A newly wed couple are getting undressed for the first time, and the husband says, **'Darling, your body is so beautiful** – let me get my camera and take a picture.' 'Why?' asks his wife. 'So that I can keep it with me always and remember how beautiful you are,' he says. Then he takes his clothes off and she says, 'Darling, I must also take a photograph of you.' 'Why?' asks her husband. **'So I can get it enlarged,'** she replies.

**What do you call a woman without
an arsehole?**

Divorced.

Why are
men **like** fine
wine?

**It takes a lot of trampling
and keeping them
in the dark before**
they mature
**into something you'd want
to have dinner with.**

What do you do if your boyfriend starts smoking?
Slow down.

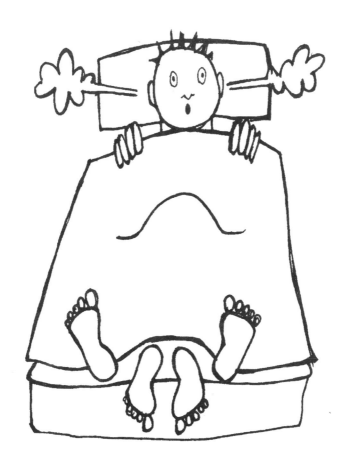

Name the disease that paralyses women below the waist?

Marriage.

If he can't get it up, you can go down, **but if he can't get it in,** get out.

A married couple answer the doorbell to find a bald gnome holding a mirror. **'This is a magic mirror,'** says the bald gnome. He hangs it on the front door and offers to demonstrate it. Rubbing his head, the gnome says, 'Mirror, mirror on the door, make me hairy as before.' With a flash, the gnome has a full head of hair. Impressed, the couple buy the mirror, take it **into the bedroom** and hang it on the bedroom door. First the woman goes up to the mirror, rubs her breasts and says, 'Mirror, mirror on the door, make my bosoms forty-four.' There's a flash, and instantly she has forty-four inch bosoms. The husband is terribly excited – he rushes over to the mirror, rubbing his cock furiously, and shouts, 'Mirror, mirror on the door, make my willy touch the floor'. **There's a huge flash**, and instantly his legs disappear.

How do married couples use Vaseline to help with their sex lives?

They put it on the bedroom doorknob to keep the kids out.

Oral sex can make your day, but anal sex can make your hole weak.

What's the difference between embarrassment, worry and panic?

Embarrassment is the first time a man can't get it up a second time.

Worry is the first time he can't get it up for the first time.

Panic is the second time he can't get it up for the first time.

What's the difference between men and fine wine?

You don't have to roll a man around in your mouth to get the most enjoyment out of him.

In Heaven, the lovers are French, the comedians are English and the engineers are German.

In Hell, the comedians are German, the engineers are French and the lovers are English.

SHAGGY
BITCH
STORIES

Three women are in the vet's waiting room with their dogs. 'What a lovely labrador,' says one, 'What are you bringing him in for?' 'He is lovely', says the owner, 'But he's a terrible chewer, he's chewed the furniture, my husband's shoes, but the final straw was when he chewed up my husband's golfclubs and left nothing but a pile of sawdust. So my husband said, either the dog goes, or he goes.' 'So you're having him put to sleep?' 'I'm afraid so' says the owner.

The second dog is a collie. 'What a lovely collie, what are you bringing him in for?' 'He is lovely but he's a terrible chaser. He chases cars, he chases bicycles, he even chases the postman. The final straw came when he chased my husband's mother down the drive and out of the gate. So my husband said, either the dog goes, or he goes.' 'So you're having him put to sleep?' 'Yes, I'm afraid so.'

So they turn to the third dog. 'What a lovely Great Dane.' 'He is lovely, but he's a terrible shagger. He'll shag anything, the sofa, the neighbour's dog, the vicar's leg. The final straw was when I was getting out of the shower. I bent over to pick up the soap and in no time he was on top of me, shagging away. It took my husband ten minutes to pull him off, and that was it — my husband said, either that dog goes, or I go.' 'So you're having him put to sleep?' 'Oh no, I've just brought him in to have his claws trimmed.'

A Hell's Angel drops his motorbike off to be mended, and is walking home. On the way he remembers that he's meant to be picking up some things at the hardware shop for the Hell's Angel Clubhouse. 'Ah, yes,' says the shopkeeper, **'Here you are,'** and he gets out a bucket, an anvil, a goat, an axe and a black cockerel. 'How am I meant to carry this lot without my bike?' **says the Hell's Angel. 'Well,' says the**

shopkeeper, 'You could put the cockerel under one arm, **the anvil under the other arm, put the axe in the bucket and hold it in one hand, then lead the goat with the other hand.' So the Hell's Angel does as the shopkeeper suggests and starts walking back to the Clubhouse. A few yards down the road, he's stopped by a little old lady. 'Excuse me, young man,' she says,** 'Can you tell me the way to the chapel?'

'It's right next to our clubhouse,' says the Hell's

Angel, 'So come with me and I'll show you the way. It's just down this alley.' The old lady looks at him very suspiciously. 'Young man,' she says, 'You are a tall, hairy, muscular man and I am a helpless old woman. How do I know you won't get me half way down that alley, push me roughly against the wall, pull down my panties and take me roughly till your wicked desires are sated?' 'Madam,' he replies, 'I have a bucket in one hand with an axe in it, a goat on a string in the other hand, an

anvil under one arm and a cockerel under the other arm, how could I possibly push you roughly against any wall?' So the old lady says, 'Put the cockerel down, **put the bucket over the cockerel and the anvil on top of the bucket, lay the axe on the ground and I'll hold on to the goat.'**

A man walks into a bar with a frog. He puts the frog on the bar and orders a pint and a packet of peanuts. Then he says, 'Billy – catch!', and throws the peanuts to the frog, one at a time, who catches them in its mouth. 'Wow,' says the barmaid, 'a performing frog!' 'Yes,' says the man, 'This frog can do all sorts of tricks. It catches peanuts, it fetches a stick – and it gives the best cunnilingus in the world.' The barmaid can't believe her ears, so the man says if she doesn't believe him, she can try it for herself. At closing time, the barmaid takes the man and the frog upstairs and lies naked on the bed. The man put the frog gently down between her legs but the frog does nothing. 'Billy – cunnilingus!' says the man. Still the frog does nothing. 'Oh for heavens sake Billy,' says the man, 'How many times do I have to show you?'

A guy gets a new sports car and takes his girlfriend out for a spin. She keeps telling him to go faster and

faster, but at around 100 miles an hour he gets a bit scared. 'If I take off my top, will you do 120?' **He says yes, so she takes off her top and he does 120.** 'If I take off all my clothes, will you do 150?' **she says. He says yes, so she takes off all her clothes, and he does 150.** 'If I give you a blow job, will you do 200?' **she says. He says yes, so she starts giving him a blow job and he puts his foot down. Before they know it, they've run off the road, she's been thrown clear and he's trapped**

**under the car with only one
foot sticking out. She tries
to pull him out, but his shoe
just comes off. 'Go and get
help!' he shouts. 'I can't,**

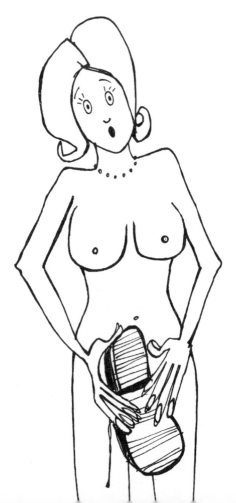

I'm naked and all my clothes are trapped under the car,' she says. But there's nothing else to be done, so she covers her privates with his shoe, runs to the nearest house and bangs on the door. An old farmer opens the door and she starts shouting, 'Please, you've got to help me, my boyfriend's stuck. Can you help me pull him out?' The old farmer looks slowly down at the shoe and says 'Nope, I reckon he's too far in for that.'

A ventriloquist is out on a country walk, and sees a farmer leaning on a gate.

'Afternoon,' says the ventriloquist. 'Afternoon,' says the farmer. Then the ventriloquist turns to the farmer's dog. 'Afternoon,' he says to the dog, and 'Afternoon,' comes the dog's reply. The farmer looks amazed, but he doesn't say anything. 'This your master?' asks the ventriloquist. 'Yep,' says the dog. 'And how does he look after you?' 'Oh, pretty well,' says the dog, 'he feeds me, he lets me sleep in the kitchen and he pats me now and then.' The farmer looks amazed, but he says nothing. 'I see you've got a horse,' says the ventriloquist, 'Mind if I talk to him?' 'Go ahead,' says the farmer. 'Afternoon,' says the ventriloquist.

'Afternoon,' the horse replies. The farmer is looking more and more surprised, but still he says nothing. 'How does the farmer look after you?' asks the ventriloquist. 'Oh, pretty well,' says the horse, 'he feeds me, I have my own stable, and he takes me out for a trot every day.' Then the ventriloquist looks into the field behind the farmer and says, 'I see you have some sheep…' 'Oh,' says the farmer, 'Those sheep are liars! Those sheep are liars!'

Four nuns die and go to Heaven. At the Pearly Gates, Saint Peter stops them. 'Before you enter Heaven, you must be completely pure,' he says. 'Sister Mary, have you ever had the slightest contact with a man's penis?' 'I must confess that I have,' says Sister Mary, 'I once saw a man's penis.' 'Wash your eyes out with this holy water and pass into Heaven,' says Saint Peter. 'Now, Sister Martha, have you ever had the slightest contact with a man's penis?' 'I must confess that I have,' says Sister

Martha, 'I once stroked a man's penis with my hand.' 'Wash your hand in this Holy Water and pass into Heaven' says Saint Peter. But before he can get any further, the other two nuns have started pushing and shoving. 'Sisters!' says Saint Peter sternly, 'There is room for all in the Kingdom of God – what is the meaning of this unseemly scuffling?' 'If I'm going to have to gargle with that Holy Water,' says the fourth nun, 'I want to get to it before Sister Catherine sticks her fat arse in it.'

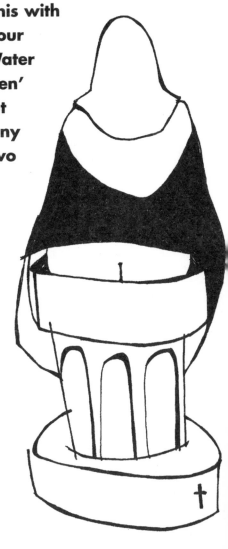

A man goes into a chemist's shop and asks to speak to a male chemist, as he has an embarrassing problem. 'I'm sorry,' says the female chemist, 'My sister and I run this shop, you'll have to speak to one of us about it.' Well, the man's very embarrassed, but he tells her that he's had a permanent hard-on for the last year and whatever he does, he can't get rid of it for more than ten minutes. 'Can you give me anything for it?' The chemist says she needs to consult her sister, and two minutes later comes back and says, 'The best we can manage is £30,000 a year and a third share of the shop.'

Tonto and the Lone Ranger are riding through the desert, when Tonto pulls up his horse and dismounts. He kneels down and presses his ear to the ground, while the Lone Ranger waits in

silence. Finally Tonto raises his head, nods wisely and speaks. 'Buffalo come.' **'Amazing,' says the Lone Ranger, 'Your Indian lore never fails to impress me. Tell me, Tonto, how can you tell?' Tonto speaks again, 'Ear sticky.'**

Two men see a dog licking his own balls. 'I wish I could do that', says the first man, 'You can,' says the second man, 'if you give him a biscuit first.'

A nun is sitting in the bath when there's a knock on the door. 'Who is it?' she says. 'It's the blind man,' comes the reply. So she thinks; that's all right, he won't see me naked and tells him to come in. The man comes in and says, 'Blimey, a naked nun. Now, where do you want this venetian blind?'

A woman goes to buy a parrot, and the shopkeeper says, 'We've got one for £100, one for £200 and one for £15.'

'Why is that one so cheap?' asks the woman. 'Well, it used to live in a brothel, so it's a bit foulmouthed.' The woman says she doesn't mind, so she pays her £15 and takes the parrot home.

As soon as she takes the cover off the cage, the parrot says, 'Fuck me, a new brothel!' Then he looks at the woman and says 'Fuck me, a new Madam.' 'I am not a Madam, and this is not a brothel,' says the woman, but she thinks it's quite

funny. Later on, her two teenage daughters come in. 'Fuck me,' says the parrot, 'New prostitutes!' 'We are not prostitutes,' say the daughters, but they think it's quite funny too. 'Wait till Dad comes in and hears this parrot, he'll go spare.' So they put the parrot in the hall, the door opens and Dad comes in. Dad looks at the parrot, and the parrot looks at him, then the parrot says, 'Fuck me, Dave, haven't seen you for weeks.'

EVERY
QUESTION
HAS AN
ANSWER

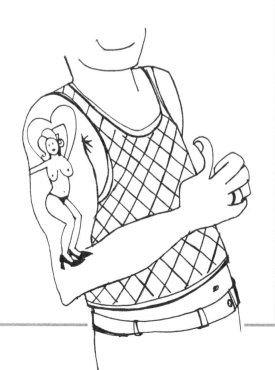

What's the difference between a forged dollar and a skinny man?

One's a phoney buck, the other's a bony fuck.

Why do men whistle on the toilet?

It helps them to remember which end to wipe.

What's the difference between a 69 and driving in fog?

When you're driving in fog, you can't see the arsehole in front of you.

Why is sex like a bungee **jump?**

It's over in no time, and if the rubber breaks you're in trouble.

Why did the **pervert** cross the road?

He couldn't get his dick out of the chicken.

What's the difference between a man and a jellybean?

Jellybeans come in different **colours.**

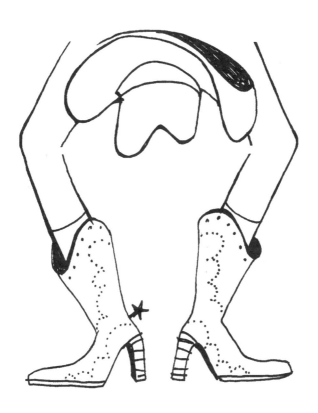

Why do cowgirls have bow legs?

Because cowboys never take their hats off, even when they're eating.

What's the difference between a man and a condom?

Condoms aren't thick and insensitive these days.

Why is a hangover better than a man?

A hangover is usually gone by lunchtime.

Why are men like cowpats?

The older they get, the easier they are to pick up.

What's the best thing about a nudist wedding?

It's easy to spot the Best Man.

What do you call a beautiful woman on the arm of an ugly man?

A tattoo.

Why is a woman like a **TV** remote control?

Because a man will just sit there pushing buttons randomly till something happens.

Why is a man like a dining table?

They both have an extra bit that extends for entertaining.

Why do bald men **have holes in their pockets?**
So they can run their fingers through their hair.

What is **warm and soft** when a man comes in drunk at night and **hard and stiff** when he wakes up in the morning?

The pile of puke at the **bottom** of the stairs.

Why is cheap lager like having sex in a canoe?

They're both fucking close to water.

What do you do to make five pounds of fat look sexy?
Put them in a push-up bra.

What's the definition of a slag?
A woman with the sexual morals of a man.

Why is car insurance cheaper
for women?

**Because women don't
get blow jobs while they're
driving.**

Why is a bloke like a computer?
You don't realise how much either of them means to
you until they go down on you.

What's the best thing
about sex with a clown?
**Great big feet, you
know what they say
about men with
big feet.**

And the worst thing?
**Infidelity: you'll catch
him having sex with
the contortionist behind
her back.**

What's the best thing about sex with a taxi driver?

He's never in a hurry to get from A to B, in fact he'll usually take as long as he can.

And the worst thing?

You can never tell when he's going to pull out.

What's the best thing about sex with a bank clerk?

The bigger the deposit and the longer you leave it in, the more interest you get.

And the worst thing?

He's not so keen on withdrawals.

What's the best thing about sex with a despatch rider?

He's dressed completely in leather and he's really, really dirty.

And the worst thing?

He's always slipping into narrow spaces where you're not meant to go.

What's the definition of an ugly man?

Even his computer won't go down on him.

What's the difference between an egg and a wank?

You can beat an egg.

PUSSY
POWER

What did the banana say to the vibrator?

I don't know why you're trembling – I'm the one she's going to eat!

How do you know who gives the best cunnilingus?
Word of mouth.

What's the difference between a genealogist and a gynaecologist? **One looks up your family tree and the other just looks up your bush.**

What's the difference between a pussy and a grill?
Nobody minds if you stab their sausage with a fork before you put it in your grill.

What's the difference between **pussy** and apple **pie?**

Any man will eat his mother's apple pie.

How does a policewoman part her hair?

(bending knees)
'Hello, hello, hello...'

Why don't women blink
during foreplay?
No time.

Why don't the sanitary towels talk to the tampons?

Because they're stuck up cunts.

Why do women have two pairs of lips?

One to talk to a man and one to shut him up.

Why do women rub their eyes in the morning?

Because they haven't got balls.

What's white, eight inches long, takes two batteries, gives complete satisfaction in three minutes and once you've tried it you'll never go back to the manual method?

An electric toothbrush.

What do you call a man with a twelve-inch tongue who can hold his breath for ten minutes?

Nothing, just keep hold of his ears.

What's the definition of a man with a long tongue? **When he sticks it our for the doctor, the nurse goes 'Aaaah!'**

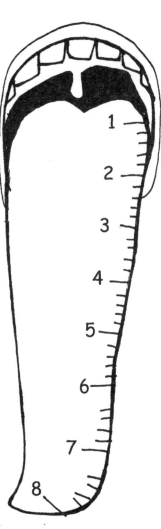

Two nuns are sitting in the bath. One says, **'Where's the soap?'** The other replies, 'Yes, it does doesn't it.'

9

WHO SAYS **BLONDES** ARE STUPID?

Why do blondes have more **fun**?

They're more easily impressed.

Why did the blonde have sex with the lights on?
She left the car door open.

How do a blonde's **brain cells die?**

Lonely.

Why do blondes make **bad** dairy farmers?

They can't keep two calves together.

Hear about the blonde girl who decided to iron the curtains?

She fell out of the window.

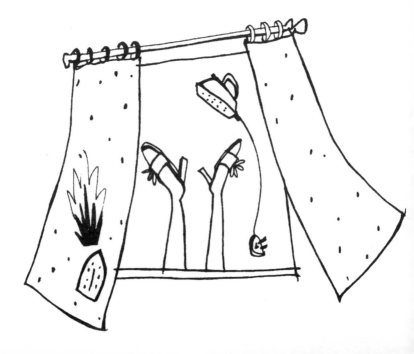

Why don't **blondes** look out of the window in the morning?

They'd have nothing to do in the afternoon.

A guy walks into a bar with a crocodile. He sits on a bar stool, gets out a big stick and hits the crocodile once around the head. The crocodile opens its mouth wide, the man unzips his fly, gets his cock out and put it in the crocodile's mouth. The man then hits the crocodile again with the stick and it gently closes its mouth, as the whole bar holds its breath.

Finally, the man gives the crocodile another sharp tap with the stick, it opens its mouth again and he takes his cock out and puts it back in his pants. 'Right,' he says, 'If anyone else wants to try that, I'll give them a hundred pounds.' Silence. Everyone stares at the crocodile.

'Come on,' says the man, 'a hundred pounds for anyone who'll do it.' Then a blonde girl pipes up from the back, **'I'll give it a try, but please don't hit me so hard with that stick.'**

Two blondes are planning a bank robbery. One of them stays in the car with the engine running and the other one pulls on a balaclava. 'Now,' says the getaway driver, 'You've got the gun?' 'Yes.' 'You've got the rope?' 'Yes.' 'And you've got the dynamite.' 'Yes.' 'Go for it!' So the blonde runs into the bank. She's been gone a long time and no explosion. Then she's been gone a very

long time and still no explosion. The getaway driver is about to give up and drive off when the blonde runs out of the bank; no money, balaclava half off, pursued by a security guard with his trousers round his ankles, and jumps in the car. As they speed off, the getaway driver says, 'I tell you every time – you're meant to tie up the guard and blow the safe.'

Two blonde girls walk into a building. You'd have thought one of them would have seen it.

A blonde, a brunette and a redhead get into a lift, and notice a white sticky patch on the wall. 'That's funny,' says the brunette, 'that looks like spunk.' The redhead sniffs the air and says, 'Yep, and it smells like spunk.' The blonde puts her finger in the sticky patch, licks her finger and says, 'Well, it's nobody from our office.'

Why is a blonde girl like a beer bottle?

They've both got nothing but air from the neck up.

What's the difference between a blonde and a road sign?
Road signs sometimes say 'Stop'.

What does a blonde do with her arsehole in the morning?
Give him his packed lunch and send him to work.

Why did the blonde swap her car for a convertible?

She wanted the extra legroom.

Three blond men find an old bottle. When they open it a genie pops out and offers them a wish each.

'Brilliant!' says the first blond, 'I'd like you to make me more intellig... intellig... not so stupid.' Bouf! There's a puff of smoke and the guy has red hair. So the second blond guy says, 'I'd like to be even more intellig... intellig... even less stupid than he is.' Bouf! Another puff of smoke, and the second guy has brown hair. So the third blond says, 'I'd like to be even more intellig... intellig... even less stupid than both my friends.' Bouf! There's a third puff of smoke and when it clears, he's still blonde, but now he's a woman.

A blonde girl has a baby, and the family all come round to visit. They ask to see the baby, but she says, **'Not yet, it's asleep.'** They wait a while and then they ask again. 'Not yet, it's asleep,' comes the answer. Finally it's getting late and they have to leave, so they ask once more to see the baby. 'Not yet, it's asleep. You have to wait till it cries,' comes the answer. 'Why do we have to wait till it cries?' they ask. 'Because I forgot where I put it down.'

What's the hardest thing to hit a blonde girl with?

A new idea.

A blonde is walking down the street with her blouse unbuttoned and her right breast hanging out. A policeman stops her and says, 'Madam – are you aware I could arrest you for indecent exposure. You can't walk along the street with your breast hanging out.' The blonde looks down and says, 'Oh goodness – I left the baby on the bus again!'

What's the difference between a **clever** blonde and a dumb blonde?

The clever blondes have dark roots showing.

What's the difference between a blonde girl and a light bulb?
The light bulb is brighter, but the blonde is easier to turn on.

How do you know when you've got a blonde gardener?

The bushes are slightly darker than the rest of the garden.

A blonde is crossing the road when a car hits her. The driver rushes over to see if she's okay. 'My eyes, my eyes,' she shouts, 'Everything's gone all blurry! I'm going blind!' The driver's worried that he might have really injured her, so he says, 'How many fingers have I got up?' 'Oh no!' she cries, 'Don't say I'm paralysed from the waist down as well!'

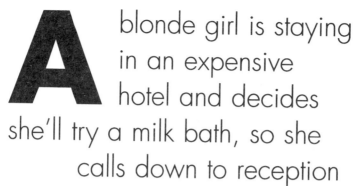

A blonde girl is staying in an expensive hotel and decides she'll try a milk bath, so she calls down to reception and asks them to send up thirty pints of milk to fill up the bath. 'Pasteurised?' asks the receptionist. 'No, just up to my tits,' replies the blonde.

Why do blondes wear knickers?

To keep their ankles warm.

What does a blonde girl do for foreplay?
Warm her ankles.

What two things in the air can get a blonde girl pregnant?
Her legs.

What's the difference between a blonde girl and the Grand Old Duke of York?

The Grand Old Duke of York only had ten thousand men.

What's the difference between a blonde girl and the Titanic?
They know how many men went down on the Titanic.

What's the difference between a blonde and a **politician**?

A blonde only screws one person at a time.

B londe girl goes to the doctor and says, 'I hurt all over.' She presses her finger into her knee 'That hurts.' Then she presses her finger into her stomach, 'That hurts,' and then she presses her finger into her forehead, 'Even that hurts. What is it, doctor?' The doctor replies, 'You have a broken finger.'

Do blondes really have more fun?
Yes, they just can't remember who with.

Hear about the blonde chef?
She thought Coq au Vin was sex in the back
of a Transit.

How many blondes does
it take to change a
light bulb?
**Just one – and
a dozen men
to look up her
skirt while she
does it.**

Hear about the other blonde chef who could only cook chicken in scrumpy sauce?
She couldn't have a cock in her hand, without wanting it in cider.

Why did the blonde girl have sunglasses inside her knickers?

The weather forecast said there would be sunny periods.

Why did the blonde girl have lipstick on her steering wheel?
She was trying to blow her horn.

Why do men call blondes 'dolls'?
Because when you lie them on their backs, their eyes close.

Why do men like blonde girl jokes?
Because they can understand them.